Making Money in the Fast Lane
Volume 1
by Art McGee

Table of Contents

1. Introduction

Thank you again for purchasing my book, I hope you enjoy reading this book and be able to learn from the information I'm giving you.Because the information in this book will change your life. I put this book together for you to enjoy and learn how to create another income. Thank you for choosing my book on how to make money.

2. Making Money in the Fast Lane Volume

Hi I'm writing this to show you how money can be made in the fast lane. I call certain stocks in the market fast lane product. You can make a little money every day or every other day. First you need to open an account with a broker, enable your **option and margin** in that account.

Different brokers require a certain amount of money to open your account. There is a website you can go to and find out about the different brokers that are available to use. Go on line and type in "**stock market**" this will bring different one's up. You may choose what is best for you at that time. If you are new and do not have a lot of money do not trade on margin. Because margin require you to keep a certain amount of money in your account it also expose all of your money in that account.

About now you are wondering how money can be made doing this type of work. I'm walk you step by step on how to trade. Some fast lane stocks have weekly options. 1 option contract is equal to 100 shares. If one contract cost you $1.00 multiply that $1.00 times 100 shares which equal to $100. There are several ways' you may trade on option. Start out buying weekly option and trade them on an **intraday level**. When you purchase an option buy it at the strike price.

3. Making Money

Strike price means if a stock is $25 that is your strike price in the money. If the stock is moving up and has a **bullish pattern** you purchase a $25 **call**. The **call option** mean the stock is going up. Give the market **15 to 25 minute** to open before you purchase any stock or option making sure the stock continues to go up. You left click on the trade panel then **left click** on the ask price and a screen will come up asking you do you want to purchase it, then you left click confirm.

If the stock continues to go up within that **15 to 45 minute**, you left click on the **monitor panel, left click on the stock** and left click to close the order or choose **trail stop within -5 to -10 cents** at **market** and left click confirm now you don't have to watch that stock, it will sell automatically. If the stock goes to a high within that 30 minute to 1 hour time frame or starts to back off. The **red volume indicator will start to appear**, go right ahead and sell that stock. When you trade on an intraday use the 5 minute intraday charts it easier to manage than a 15 minute intraday chart. You try to find a stock that has a good pattern; these are the ones that buck the market.

The **Put Option** means the stock is going down, example $25 stock go to $24. You may use the same principal when purchasing **put option** in a **bear market**. **Bull** mean the market is going up, **Bear** mean the market is going down.

4. Making Money

If you decide to buy the stock right out this means purchasing the stock at its price. A $10 stock will cost you $1000 if you purchase 100 shares. **Don't short a stock if you are new, because if you short it and the stock reverse on you money will come directly out the account.** If you decide to buy weekly option don't hold them more than two days. **Don't buy weekly option on Thursday or Friday unless it an intraday trade.**

The weekly option loses four percent each day. Make sure you close the weekly option by Thursday that is why I use the weekly option as an intraday trade. Making a slow nickel is better than a fast dime. **The reason you want your option and margin enabled because this will allow your money to go directly into the account when the stock or option are sold.** Remember, there are risks in buying stocks or options.

For example, if you decide to buy an option and the expiration day is coming up and you don't close it out, you will loose only the money you put up. This is why you purchase one stock at a time. When you buy an option contract or the stock and the stock start to go against you get out of it. The account will show negative until that stock turns around. It will be up to you if you decide to hold it or sell the stock.

5. Making Money

If you don't have $25,000 or more in your account, you can only make 3 intraday trades in 5 days. The fast lane stocks are $100 or more, sometime you may find a stock that is cheaper and move well. **All the fast lane stocks don't go up the same time each day.** I make my money on options using fast lane stocks. I'm going to draw some charts and show you how money can be made and what I do. This is a guide showing you how to get started in making money.

The market is higher today because people around the world are investing in the U. S. market. Some analysts try to predict which way the market is going. This is hard to do because today's market is news driven. The market does what it wants' don't try to buck the market take what it give you. Be like a pine tree that moves with the direction of the wind. When a stock break out the first day from being down for so many days, follow it to the upside long as possible or put a trail stop market order in. This will allow you to do something else while trail stop is working.

Always trade to make a successful trade not to make money. If you make a successful trade the money will follow. **Don't let a winning trade turn into a loosing trade take your profit.** Sometime you may buy stocks at the wrong time that alright just regroups and try it again. **Make sure you look at the stock in premarket to see what it's doing.**

6. Making Money

Some stocks don't trade in premarket; you may have to wait 15 to 25 minute to see which direction those stocks are going. Take control of your own financial empire, because making money in the fast lane is like fishing or hunting. **Some time you may have to wait 30 minute to 1 hour before the stock you are trading moves to it peak. Before you purchase any stock or option checks the volume, because that what move each stock.**

The market gaps up and down some morning doing premarket; it's hard to trade because of the gap. The **Federal Reserve speaks** sometime and the market goes sideways. The stocks stay in a certain range doing that time. If you haven't made a good trade within the **30 to 60 minute time frame,** wait until that evening to trade. Sometime it's good to take a few days off to refresh your mind. If you work in the day time use a cell phone or I Pad to make trades unless you have access to a computer. **If the market keep chopping around and you haven't made any money within a 1 to 1 ½ hour time frame wait until that evening. If the market doesn't change wait until the next day.**

Sometime the markets go down and certain stocks go up, you need to look and see what making that stock go up. **If you don't catch that stock at the beginning don't chase it.** You may desire to make a **swing trade or a basic window trade**. A swing trade is when a stock hit lows or highs. A basic window trade is similar; example let say a certain stock hit an all time high.

7. Making Money

You want to see if that stock continues to go up, monitor that stock 3 to 5 trading session. You want to use this same principal when a stock hit it lows. Once that stock hit a certain area high or low set an alerts to warn you when it move in either direction. Also when you purchase a stock make sure you put a **stop limit marker order** on that stock. Example let say you purchase a $25 call option; you put a $24.75 stop limit marker order in. Remember if you haven't made money that morning within 1 to 1 ½ hour time frame do not buy any stock wait until that evening.

I'm drawing charts in volume 2 explaining in more detail; they are guides showing you what to look for. **If you haven't made any money within that first 1 to 1 1/2 hour don't buy anything unless you see something pop to the upside or downside.** When that stock peak out at the **upside** or **downside** sell it. Sometime when you make a good profit it good to transfer the money back to your bank account and wait a while before you trade again. If you need to make a certain amount of money don't trade that day, let your mind settle down for a while before you trade. When you trade look and see what direction the market is going. Some stocks buck the trend of the market.

Sometime the market just chops around and builds value in a certain area, if the market does that wait until that evening or the next day to trade. **Value means** most of the volume is in a certain area. Before you trade a stock do some research on that stock to learn its pattern? **Remember to make your money in the morning or that evening. If you buy a stock on an intraday trade and its very bullish ride that stock as long as you can that day before you sell it.** If the market continuing moving higher most of the high flying stock will run a least 2 days. **If you decide to make a swing trade on weekly option make sure you are out of them by Thursday.**

8. On Option

On option expiration week; most stock stay in a certain range so if you buy weekly option do not hold them no **more than 2 days.** When you buy option make sure that option is paying good. **If the call side is red and the put side is red at the same time on the price grid don't trade that stock. The price grid is located under trade panel, you want to trade option if the call side is green and the put side is red are the put side is green and call side is red. Find you 2 to 3 stocks to trade starting out, make sure you learn the pattern for each stock.**

If you are trading a stock on intraday look at the intraday 2 day 5 minute chart. This will let you see what the stock has done in 2 days. You also want to bring up the 5 day 5 minute chart for the past 5 days. You also want to bring up the daily chart to see what it do. Bring up the daily 6 month 5 minute chart to see what happen in the last 6 month. On your trade platform click the minute button to change each time set. When you set the intraday click style, then move your cursor to today then click 5 minute spot. When you decide to trade use a 1 day intraday 5 minute chart, this will allow you to make money in the morning or afternoon. If you trade in the morning, the stock will go up or down. Give the market 15 to 25 minute to open before you purchase any stock. If that stock hit a peak going up or down wait for the opposite volume change to come in before you sell that stock. **When you buy a put option make sure that stock is not paying dividend in the next 5 days.**

9. Making Money

Some of you work during the day; you may get a chance to work some swing trade on a weekly or monthly basic. When Thursday and Friday come try to trade stocks coming off earning or upgrade and downgrade. Sometime stocks hit a 3 or 5 day resisted point then turns around. Sometime companies make deals and those stocks go up, these are the ones you want to trade.

You don't need a college education to open an account to trade stocks. **The market pulls back most of the time doing option expiration Friday.** Make sure you sell those weekly options by 12:00 noon on Friday, because option value decreases more after 12:00 noon time. Remember if you work in the day time come home and do your homework before you trade. **Caution make sure when you trade weekly option try to trade them on an intraday level. If you buy them in the money and hold it for the next day you lose 4% the next day.**

If you have purchase a call or put option for a certain price, example 0.30 x 100 shares equal $30. If you don't think you will sell it on time before expiration put an order to sell it at 0.30 or more with good until cancel limit order. This will keep the broker from charging you a service fee for an expired option.

10. Round Trip and making money

Do not buy a weekly option on Wednesday unless you are doing a round trip.
This book was writing for the consumer to take charge of their financial life. I want you to get motivated and learn how to take cure of yourself and family. I'm not asking you to quit your job but learn how to set up an extra income. You should be able to find fast lane stock from the internet or shows that talk about stocks.

When you invest it may involves great risk. This information is for you to obtain and not guarantee to work 100 % of the time but is great information. The information provided here is for educational purposes only. You should make all of the investment decision and do your own research. The information provided is through hand on experience trading in the market. Remember if a stock has traded up 2 days in a row, then the 3rd day that stock go up when the market first open give the stock 15 to 25 minute to see if it continuing to go up before you purchase it again. Most stocks usually back off the 3rd day.

11. Making Money

Remember when buying option make sure you make your money in the morning or that evening. Do not buy an option after the market has been open (1 ½ to 2) hour in the morning. The stock market usually pulls back or goes sideways doing that time and option value pull back doing that time. If you decide to purchase a swing trade or basic window trade wait until the market pull back that evening before you purchase an option on a swing or basic window trade.

You can always search the internet for other information to help you understand. Buying option are different from purchasing stock right out. When buying option try to purchase the stock that move $1 to $ 2 within a day. Make sure you purchase the stock that has a 0.50 to $1 increment. Example you purchase a $100 stock that move to $101, $102 …etc on the price grid. These are the one you look for. Make sure you read this entire book and study the charts before you trade any stock.

Trading stocks is like being in a fist fight; you need to know what your next move is. Make sure you click the analyze panel to see how much that stock will go up within the week under probability analysis.I want you to be looking for my volume 2 keeping you updated on the market.Remember you need to give the market 15 to 25 minute opening time before you trade.One hour before the market open look to see if the index are high or low. This will give you an ideal which way the market is going.If the market index are high one hour before opening it a good chance the market will sell off are go sideways.If the market index are low one hour before opening it a good chance the market will go up   are go sideways.

12. Trading Rules

Rule one; do your research before any trade is made.

Rule two; trade only 1 stock at a time.

Rule three; make your money in the morning or that evening.

Rule four; take what the market give you and do not force a trade.

Rule five; do not chase a stock after it has run up.

Rule six; give the market 15 to 25 minute when it open before you trade.

Rule seven; beware of a choppy market.

Rule eight; if the market is going sideways do not trade.

Rule nine; take your profit.

Rule ten; do not trade if you need to make money that day, wait until the next day after you have relax you mind.

13. Glossary

Stock Option: A privilege, sold by one party to another, that gives the buyer the right, but not the obligation, to buy (call) or sell (put) a stock at an agreed-upon price within a certain period or on a specific date.

Margin: Borrowed money that is used to purchase securities. This practice is referred to as "buying on margin".

Call option: The period of time between the opening and closing of some future markets wherein the prices are established through an auction process. Option contract give the owner the right (but not the obligation) to buy a specified amount of an underlying security at a specified price within a specified time.

Put option: are stock market device which gives the owner of the put, the right, but not the obligation, to sell an asset (the underlying), at a specified price (the strike), by a predetermined date (the expiry or maturity) to a given party (the seller of the put). Put options are used in the stock market to protect against the decline of the price of a stock below a specified price.

14. Glossary

Candle bars: it green or red on a stock chart, when it green that mean the price increase on a stock and when red the price decrease.

Monitor panel: the word monitor is writing on your trading platform.

Trail stop: A stop order that can be set at a defined percentage away from a security's current market price. A trailing stop for a long position would be set below the security's current market price; for a short position, it would be set above the current price. A trailing stop is designed to protect gains by enabling a trade to remain open and continue to profit as long as the price is moving in the right direction, but closing the trade if the price changes direction by a specified percentage.

Stop-limit: is an order to sell or buy a stock once it reaches a certain level, but only if the shareholder can obtain a specified price.

Volume indicator: A technical indicator that measures the amount of money flowing in and out of an asset. The underlying assumption of this indicator is that there is buying pressure when the price trades near the asking price green and selling pressure when it trades near the bid red.

15. Glossary

Price Grid: All stocks in the U.S. have been quoted in decimals, rather than fractions, as a result, bid-ask spreads have contracted dramatically. Price grid is part of your trading platform.

Swing Trade: A style of trading that attempts to capture gains in a stock within 3 to 5 days. Swing traders use technical analysis to look for stocks with short-term price momentum.

Basic Window Trade: A basic window trade monitors certain stock that hit an all time high or low. You monitor that stock 3 to 5 trading session, if the stock start dropping from it high. You buy a put when trading option and short it when purchasing the stock. You may use the same principal when a stock start going up from it low.

Value means: most of the volume is in a certain area, before you trade a stock do some research on that stock to learn its pattern.

Trade panel: the word trade is writing on your trading platform.

16. Glossary

Round Trip: A round trip occurs in trading when you open and close a position in the same trading day. Example you buy 100 shares of a stock and sell 100 shares of that same stock within that day = 1 round trip Round trips are an important thing to consider as for you not violate the rules related to pattern day trading. To have more than 3 round trips in 5 business days requires you to have a margin account with at least 25,000 in equity and be designated as a pattern day trader. If you have an account less than 25,000 dollars and wish to keep your day trades at no more than 3 in a 5 business day period.

Intraday: mean a price movement of a given security over the course of one day of trading. It is generally used to describe the high and low price of a stock during a given trading day or operation.

Cover Call: is an income-producing strategy where you sell, or "write", call options against shares of stock you already own. Typically, you'll sell one contract for every 100 shares of stock. In exchange for selling the call options, you collect an option premium. But that premium comes with an obligation. If the call option you sold is exercised by the buyer, you may be obligated to deliver your shares of the underlying stock.

17. Glossary

Stock market: is the aggregation of buyers and sellers (a loose network of economic transactions, not a physical facility or discrete entity).

The Federal Reserve: often referred to as the" the Fed," is the central bank of the United States. It was created by the Congress to provide the nation with a safer, more flexible, and more stable monetary and financial system.

Index: They are the 3 different market,NASDAQ,Dow Jones and SPX 500.

18. Rules

Rules ; After you make a good profit transfer some of the funds to your bank account.

Rules; Make sure you are well rested.

Rules; When trading get in a quiet area.

Rules; When you buy a stock on intraday it over the trend line.

Rules; Beware when an analysis or bank upgrade a stock.

19. **Rules**

Rules; They upgrade stocks for you to buy then they sell them.

Rules; Please do not hold on to a loosing trade.

Rules; Try to stay flexible at all time and be ready for anything.

Rules; Do your home work the day before you trade.

20. Inclosing

I want to personally thank everyone for purchasing my book on how to make extra income and hope you learn each chapter so you may be able to make money. If you follow these guide line and learn them you will make money. I'm will be making volume 2 on chart reading explaining the directing on each chart. Thank you again.

Art

www.ingramcontent.com/pod-product-compliance
Lightning Source LLC
Chambersburg PA
CBHW070231210526

45168CB00019B/1743